THE GOLD GUIDES

PALERMO
AND
MONREALE

🄱🄱 BONECHI

© Copyright by CASA EDITRICE BONECHI
Via Cairoli 18b - 50131 Firenze, Italia
Tel. +39 055576841 - Fax +39 0555000766
E-mail: bonechi@bonechi.it - Internet: www.bonechi.it

Project and editorial conception: Casa Editrice Bonechi
Project Manager: Serena de Leonardis
Graphic design: Federica Balloni
Picture research: Sonia Gottardo
Videolayout: Federica Balloni
Cover: Laura Settesoldi
Editing: Simonetta Giorgi
Translation: Eve Leckey and Stephanie Johnson (pages 91-95)

Text: Patrizia Fabbri
Map: LAC (Litografia Artistica Cartografica)

Printed in Italy by Centro Stampa Editoriale Bonechi.

Photographs from the archives of Casa Editrice Bonechi taken by Andrea Fantauzzo.
Other contributors: Paolo Abbate, photographs pages 4, 21 below, 23 below, 24 above right
and below left, 30 above and in the centre, 31 above, 36 below, 37 below, 38, 39, 42 above
and below, 47, 53 above, 55, 66 above, 68 below;
Gianni Dagli Orti, photographs pages 24 in the centre and below right, 64 above;
Enzo Loverso, photographs pages 73-88;
Andrea Pistolesi, photographs pages 11-16, 52 above and in the centre.

The Publisher would like to thank Franco Bertolino and Mimmo Cuticchio
for their valuable consultancy.

ISBN 88-476-0672-1

* * *

INTRODUCTION

Surrounded by the sea, the lemon groves of the Conca d'Oro and the headland of Monte Pellegrino, Palermo is not only the administrative centre of the independent Region set up in 1947, but is today Sicily's only true city - the centre of the island's economic, political and cultural life. The city's present importance is the result of many centuries of history much influenced by its fortunate geographical position. Although man inhabited the slopes of Monte Pellegrino as early as the Paleolithic age, it was not until the 8th century B.C. that the Phoenicians first made use of the natural inlet now known as La Cala. Some 500 metres deeper at the time, it rapidly became one of the foremost ports in the entire Mediterranean. Since then the port has been a constant driving force not only for the island's economy, but in the history of the city of Palermo. The city takes its name from the port (Palermo is derived from "Panormus", meaning "a large port", an expression of Greek etymology which reveals the close links between the two populations, although the Greeks never conquered the island). It was through the port that the island came into contact with the most advanced civilizations, developing a thoroughly cosmopolitan character, while due to its commercial and strategic importance, the city enjoyed long and stable good fortune, protected and encouraged through centuries of history by various different cultures. The Phoenicians were succeeded in the 5th century B.C. by the Carthaginians, in turn replaced in 254 B.C. by the Romans who turned the fortified city around the port into a flourishing municipality. Following four centuries during which Vandals, Ostrogoths, Longobards and Byzantines rapidly succeeded one another, the Arab conquest in 831 brought a new period of magnificent splendour to Palermo. With the creation of new streets and buildings huddled close around the port, the original centre began to grow and the network of alleys and lanes that still exists there today is one of the few remaining indications that this was once one of the richest markets in the Mediterranean area. Before long the town acquired a notably Arab character, with mosques, splendid palaces, thriving markets and, on becoming the capital of an autonomous state in 948, an

The famous Annunciation *by Antonello da Messina.*

emir was installed here. It did not, however, extend beyond the "Paleapoli", the fortified city which today forms the historic centre of Palermo, although the area obviously also has buildings and monuments dating from the dynasty which succeeded the Arabs. In

3

1072 Robert of Normandy conquered the island, and in 1130 Roger II was crowned king of Sicily. Under Norman rule, ending with the magnanimous king William II, the extensive rebuilding which took place within the city represented an architectural rebirth. The Normans were succeeded by the Swabian king, Henry VI. His son by Constance, the last ruler of the Norman dynasty, was a splendid and cultured sovereign who created a magnificent court in Palermo, a veritable and unrivalled centre for the literature, sciences and arts of an entire epoch. In 1266 the Angevins took over the island but their ill-managed and arrogant rule lead to the bloody Sicilian Vespers revolt in 1282 and brought about the seizure of power by the Aragonese. The powerful feudal families now began to play a predominant role, building not only magnificent palaces (such as Palazzo Chiaramonte) but also grand new convents for the mendicant orders thus transforming the entire appearance of the city. The greatest transformation was, however, to take place from the beginning of the 16th century when the Spanish viceroy was installed. The subsequent architectural and urban reorganization involved administrative buildings as well as public areas. The city was divided into four ecclesiastical areas, and churches, monasteries, palazzi, as well as fountains and monuments were built to enhance the new streets and squares. This continued even after the arrival of the Bourbons in 1734 though it was not until a century later that Palermo grew beyond the confines of the old fortified city, expanding outwards, following the enlargment of the port. During the 20th century, expansion continued towards the north, to Mondello, now the favourite local beach. Today, despite Palermo's busy, modern appearance and the progressive desertion of the historic centre, seriously damaged by the earthquake of 1968, the spirit of the city is still a synthesis of this complex, historical background and is most vividly reflected in the lively and colourful local traditions as seen not only in the processions, the triumphal decorated carts and the lively local festivals, but more especially in those unique figures, the ballad singers, with their fascinating naive illustrations, the brightly painted carts which still enliven the city streets and squares, and the renowned Puppet Theatre where knights and paladins are realistically brought to life, once more to triumph over the Arab infidel, and perhaps unwittingly representing a piece of history which still survives, hidden in the depths of a communal memory.

PORTA NUOVA

The classic approach to the historic centre of Palermo is proudly heralded by the grandiose and highly original **Porta Nuova**, standing beside the solemn grandeur of Palazzo dei Normanni. Reaching Corso Vittorio Emanuele from Corso Calatafimi, one passes through the massive structure of this city gate which replaced an earlier 15th-century entrance. The Porta Nuova was built in 1583 to celebrate and immortalize the triumphal entrance into the city of Charles V almost fifty years earlier, after his participation in the defeat of Tunis in 1535.

Mannerist in style, the gate has a graceful loggia and is crowned by an unusual maiolica dome. The lower section is decorated with four impressive telamons, a recurrent feature in Renaissance and Baroque architecture, and unfortunately suffered serious damage in the past, leading to radical restoration of the entire building in 1669.

The impressive Porta Nuova, and above, a detail showing two of the four telamons.

The 17th-century façade of Palazzo dei Normani.

Below, the marble coat of arms that decorates the main entrance, and right, the grand doorway.

PALAZZO DEI NORMANNI

It is probable that some Punic and Roman fortifications once stood in the historic centre of Palermo. During the 9th century the Arabs replaced these with a powerful fortress, also known as the Emirates' Palace, which the Normans later transformed into a sumptuous residence, richly decorated by skilful Arab and Byzantine craftsmen. Thereafter it was the seat of the rulers of Sicily and their families and it was here that Frederick II of Swabia, a powerful and enlightened king, as well as a cultured lover of the arts, held his famous court where poets, scientists, philosphers and writers always had place of honour. However, the role of the palace as a political and administrative centre for the island gradually diminished with the decline of the Swabian dynasty. This lead to its partial abandonment and progressive deterioration until, with the establishment of Spanish rule

and the restoration of the building as official residence for the viceroys during the 16th century, radical rebuilding became necessary and the entire structure was reorganized, finally becoming the building we see today. **Palazzo dei Normanni**, austere and compact with its solemn 17th-century façade, designed for the viceroy Vigliena after 1616 and altered over the next two centuries, stands alongside Porta Nuova; the piazza in front is dominated by the Baroque monument to Philip V. The impressive Torre Pisana to the right of the main entrance, is an original Norman structure, today housing the astronomical observatory founded in 1786 by Giuseppe Piazzi. In 1921 the Ministero della Pubblica Istruzione (Ministery of Education) initiated a programme of research and study preliminary to the restoration of parts of the original Norman palace still in existence. This brought to light a network of passageways, once lit by torches, and a fascinating Treasury containing four large jars sunk into the floor which, at the height of the power of the Norman and Swabian rulers, probably contained an incalculable fortune in gold coins. As a result of the programme of restoration, many fascinating rooms came to light, such as the gloomy prisons and the Sala degli Armigeri (Guard's Room) with its beautiful cross vault, and a clearer idea of the original structure emerged. However, the most impressive rooms remained those for long admired and renowned, in particular the magnificent Sala di Ruggero. On the second floor, this hall is magnificently decorated with a series of mosaics covering the upper part of the walls, the vaults and the arches. Dating from 1170 the delicate, geometric designs of the mosaics echo the influence of oriental decoration and represent elegant hunting scenes with animals, plants, men and mythological figures, all portrayed with great expertise and subtlety. The overall effect is quite stunning and this magnificent hall is the most jealously guarded of all the splendours in the Palace. The Sala di Ruggero is an integral part of the wing which once housed the royal appartments, consisting of a series of magnificent rooms, such as the dining hall, pure and linear with its elegant Gothic arches recalling its original function as an atrium, the refined Sala Gialla (Yellow Room), the more theatrical Sala Rossa (Red Room), the Sala dei Viceré (Viceroy's Room), and especially the Salone di Ercole (Hercules), dating from the 16th-century but magnificently frescoed in 1799 by Giuseppe Velasquez.
Today the Regional Assembly of Sicily, the island's parliamentary assembly, meets here.

A general view of the palace including part of the piazza.

The south-west façade of Palazzo dei Normanni where the sombre yet elegant style is most evident.

Below, the splendid gardens in front of Palazzo dei Normanni with the statue of Philip V in the centre.

THE GARDENS

One of the most pleasant features of the residences of Arab Emirs, later continued by the Norman and Swabian rulers in their palaces, was the creation of extensive and luxuriant gardens. Plants flourished around artificial ponds, fountains and waterfalls, providing cool shade in delightfully refreshing oases for the ruling family and their court and guests. At the height of its splendour, Palermo's royal palace also had a superb **park**.

When the building declined through neglect, so too did the gardens, but today their original charm has been at least partly restored, providing a delightful setting for the rather austere façade of the Palazzo dei Normanni amidst cool, elegant gardens.

THE COURTYARDS

Palazzo dei Normanni is an impressive structure composed of a series of spacious internal **courtyards** surrounded by the various wings of the building. Each courtyard has its own individual character, with singular and unusual features. In particular, the elegant architectural design of the Maqueda Courtyard, named for one of the viceroys of old, is a pleasant and tranquil haven with three rows of arches, one above the other, and fine loggias. Along the upper part of the courtyard walls a delightful mosaic decoration is framed by a second row of slender columns, crowned by elegant carved capitals and deep ogives formed by the arches. The Cortile della Fontana (Fountain Courtyard) is also worth a visit; although somewhat more neglected, its architectural structure and overall elegance are equally attractive.

Views showing the sophisticated grace of the Maqueda courtyard.

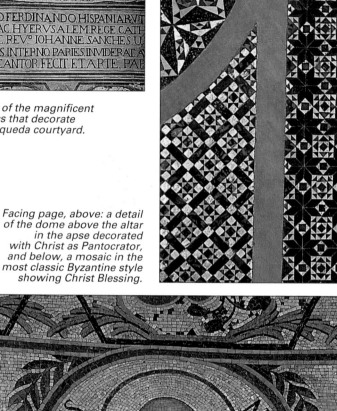

Details of the magnificent mosaics that decorate the Maqueda courtyard.

Facing page, above: a detail of the dome above the altar in the apse decorated with Christ as Pantocrator, and below, a mosaic in the most classic Byzantine style showing Christ Blessing.

THE PALATINE CHAPEL

One of the original structures, and lasting evidence of the magnificence and splendour of life within Palazzo dei Normanni, is without doubt the superb **Cappella Palatina** (Palatine Chapel), with its glittering and shining mosaics. Work on building the chapel, intended for the private use of the ruling family, began in 1130 when Roger II was crowned king of Italy, and was completed some thirteen years later as can be seen from the date 1143 given in an inscription in the dome as the year of its consecration. The plan is that of a basilica with a raised presbytery and nave and two aisles divided by rows of granite columns, crowned with elaborate, attractively gilded Corinthian capitals, while the floors, balustrades and walls are richly decorated. It is, however, the magnificent mosaic work which the visitor finds most beautiful and impressive. The typically Islamic wooden ceiling, one of the oldest to have survived until now, is also worth close attention for the extreme delicacy of the Arabian-style decorative detail. The most unusual feature here is the representation of human figures, at the time an innovation derived from Persian influences and accepted only by a few schools in the 12th century. The use of figures,

Overleaf, the altar and the vault in the apse of the Palatine Chapel, and the dome above the altar.

however, was only found in certain areas generally on the periphery of the Arab world, such as, indeed, Palermo. The highlight of the elaborate wooden ceiling, however, is undoubtedly the superb dome decorated with a mosaic image of Christ as Pantocrator, surrounded by a choir of angels and full figures of the four Evangelists. These are the oldest mosaics in the entire Palatine Chapel and may also be dated around 1143, though numerous other equally attractive mosaics decorate the walls of the transept as well as the nave and the aisles and the arches rising above the the capi-

The paschal candelabra in porphery, malachite and gold that stands to the right of the magnificent raised pulpit.

tals of the columns. The subjects, figures and people portrayed in these immense mosaic cycles are based on stories from the Old and New Testaments, with the emphasis on the life of Jesus. The large image of Christ Blessing in the rounded vault in the apse is highly evocative, standing above a sorrowing and touching figure of the Virgin Mary, while on the partition wall is a delicate Annunciation portrayed in the most classical manner. On both sides of the apse at the end of the aisles, following a traditional pattern, the mosaic images represent Saint Peter and Saint Paul. However, due to the influence of the classically Byzantine style, evident throughout the chapel, the frequent motifs of plants, vegetation and stylized figures of animals reflect a more typically Arab decoration. The Palatine Chapel is an example of superb artistry which has fascinated illustrious personalities for centuries, including Maupassant who immortalized its beauty with his praises. More than anything, however, the chapel is lasting evidence of the deeply religious nature of Sicily's Norman rulers.

Below, mosaic on the inner façade showing Christ with Saints Peter and Paul and two details of the exquisite inlay work which decorates the image.

15

Two views highlighting the beautiful mosaic images
that decorate the walls of the naves.

THE ORLÉANS PARK

Behind Palazzo dei Normanni, near what was once the centre of "Paleapoli", the fortified city which formed the original nucleus of Palermo, is Palazzo d'Orléans. This elegant building now houses the administrative offices of the Sicilian Region and is located in a large **park**, rich with luxuriant vegetation and one of the most lovely natural areas in the entire city. The park is quite charming with its ponds, attractive flowerbeds, hedges and small woods filled with many varieties of trees and bushes. A vast, verdant oasis, it lies behind Corso Re Ruggero providing views of incomparable beauty, a scenic delight and a pleasure to relax in.

The verdant Orléans Park, an oasis of luxuriant vegetation in the centre of Palermo.

Two details of San Giovanni degli Eremiti showing the unmistakeable red domes in pure oriental style.

S. GIOVANNI DEGLI EREMITI

One of the most typically Norman monuments in the city, **San Giovanni degli Eremiti** (Saint John of the Hermits) was built in 1136 by Roger II over a mosque dating from the period of Arab domination. The new church was the crowning glory of a somewhat austere monastery destined, however, to acquire great wealth and enormous power in a short period as a result of the privileges granted by the sovreign. The abbot of the monastery was also chaplain and confessor of the king and, dignified as a bishop, was called on to celebrate the most important masses in the Palatine Chapel. Roger also decreeed that all members of the royal family should be buried in the cemetery of the monastry, although no such burials actually took place. The delightful late 12th-century cloisters, where the monks would walk and meditate, are enclosed by a series of slender and elegant paired columns with an attractive well in the centre. However, the most interesting building of the entire complex is the church itself. A small structure, it consists of a single, unadorned space, with immense transversal arches and evident traces of the mosaics and tiles which once decorated the interior. There are also numerous remains, especially at roof level, of the earlier mosque, which must have adjoined the side of the present transept where some sections of frescoes are still visible. Today, however, the exterior of the building is more worthy of note, with its quite unmistakable five ochre domes over the austere, square central structure, and the solid bell tower, lightened by large, airy openings at the top. The domes are clear evidence of the Arab origin of the church's builders and designer. The entire monastery is surrounded by luxuriant gardens and fragrant exotic plants, orange trees, jasmin, roses, creating a delightful oasis and providing a particularly apt setting for a monument so typically oriental in style.

The remaining cloisters, and below, the spartan interior of San Giovanni degli Eremiti.

THE CATHEDRAL

The history of the splendid **cathedral of Palermo**, dedicated to the Blessed Virgin, is echoed in its centuries-long architectural and artistic development; it consequently reflects better than any other building the various historical epochs and events which affected the life of the city. Its overall stylistic and structural harmony does not, however, seem to have been adversely affected by these alterations and additions. Founded in 1184 by archbishop Gualtiero Offamilio (Walter of the Mill) on the site of an early Christian basilica which had been converted into a mosque by the Arabs, it was later restored to the Christian cult by the Normans. Three splendid apses formed part of the plan of the early basilica and today represent one of the few remaining original elements. Standing between two fine, slender turrets, the apses are typically Norman in style and decoration, with intertwining arches, delicate inlay work, suspended arches, curved double lintels and characteristic rounded crenellations, all enhanced by delicate and subtle colouring. The main façade of the church has always been on the west side, today facing onto Via Bonello, and its present arrangement dates from the 14th and 15th centuries. Also enclosed by two splendid towers with small columns flanking mullioned openings, the façade has a magnificent Gothic portal, though the original wooden doors were replaced in 1961 by a bronze pair designed by Filippo Sgarlata. An aedicule containing an admirable 15th-century Madonna crowns the doorway. Two extensive Gothic arcades with double arched lintels run along Via

The portico on the south side of the cathedral, and above, the 18th-century statue of Saint Rosalia banishing the plague from Messina.

Bonello, forming a somewhat unusual link between the façade and the belltower behind. Solid and square in the lower medieval section, the belltower is more finely decorated and finished in the upper section with a rather sophisticated crowning element of small turrets and the recurrent motif of little arches, a 19th-century addition by Emanuele Palazzotto.

The south side of the cathedral is also a mixture of styles; an elegant portico with three Gothic arches, built around 1430 by Antonio Gambara in Catalan-Gothic style is enclosed by two low turrets. The first column on the left must have been part of the church which existed before the cathedral and later transformed into a mosque, as a passage from the Koran is engraved on it. Also below the portico, crowned by a tympanum decorated with oriental motifs, and solemnly guarded by statues of the four evangelists standing in niches on either side, is an ornate doorway with typically Gothic features, also by Gambara. The south side faces onto the splendid Piazza della Cattedrale, with its flourishing palm trees, constructed for archbishop Simone da Bologna in the 15th century, and improved by the addition, a century later, of the marble fountain and rather theatrical balusters supporting statues of saints, which form a decorative enclosure around the square. The fountain too has a highly expressive allegorical group of sculptures which dominate it from on high. Commissioned in 1744 by Ignazio Sebastiano

One of the statues of the four evangelists located in the niches in the portico on the south side, and below, an external view of the area of the apse.

21

The neo-classical interior of the cathedral and the small chapel dedicated to Saint Rosalia, where the remains of Palermo's protectress are housed.

Gravina, prince of Belmonte, the group includes a figure of Saint Rosalia banishing the plague from Messina. At the time when this sculptural group was added, the old fountain, known since time immemorial as the "Fountain of the Three Old Men" (Fontana dei Tre Vecchioni), was replaced with the present elegant and more graceful structure. The north side of the building shows, more than any other, the result of the various, successive alterations which the entire building has undergone. An example of these changes and additions is the 16th-century portico, almost certainly designed by Gagi-

ni, which not only had a new doorway added in 1659, but was entirely incorporated into the substantial rebuilding carried out in 1781. The large Baroque dome was also added in 1781 as part of the radical renovation carried out by Ferdinando Fuga, whose intervention is clearly evident throughout the building as he also transformed the original plan of the basilica into that of a Latin cross, adding the side aisles and the wings of the transept.

Until 1801, therefore, the interior continued to undergo modifications which produced the Neoclassic, but rather frigid, harmony seen today. Along the nave, and part of the previous basilica, are pilasters composed of four columns. Numerous statues by Francesco Laurana and Antonio Gagini are now placed around these pilasters while various other sculptural elements by Gagini and his collaborators are found elsewhere in the building. The right aisle is of particular interest as the tombs of famous emperors and kings are housed there: Roger II and Henry VI who died in 1154 and 1197 respectively; the Roman sarcophagus containing the remains of Constance of Aragon; the tombs of Frederick II and Constance, the empress daughter of Roger II; the funerary urn of Peter of Aragon; the sarcophagus of William, Duke of Athens, who died in 1338. Of great

antiquity are the majestic wooden Catalan-Gothic choir stall dated 1466, the bishop's seat and the pasqual candelabra with a 12th-century mosaic decoration. Dominating the altar in the left transept is a most beautiful 13th-century wooden Crucifix, clearly Gothic in style, originally in the church of San Niccolò la Kalsa. In the right transept is the Chapel of Saint Rosalia, patron of Palermo, where her bones are preserved in a magnificent solid silver urn.

The atmospheric 12th-century crypt of the cathedral is also rather interesting, the original Norman structure remaining almost unaltered here. A series of granite columns forms two transversal naves, one of which has seven recesses each with a cross vaulted roof. The crypt houses many tombs dating from Roman, Byzantine, Norman or later periods, and containing the remains of notable personalities. Gualtiero Offamilio (Walter of the Mill), the founder of the cathedral, is buried

Two statues of saints decorating the pilasters in the nave and a detail of the magnificent high altar.

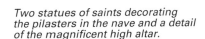

Rare items in the Cathedral
Treasury: a 16th-century altar
frontal which belonged
to Archbishop Carandolet,
an 18th-century liturgical
vestment, a gold tiara which
belonged to Catherine
of Aragon, a 13th-century glass
container of Sicilian-Arab
manufacture and a detail
of a cope showing the baptism
of Saint Ninfa (18th-century).

here. The front nave of the crypt is now partially obscured by the base of the apse of the cathedral above.

Situated in a separate room, the Treasury (Tesoro della Cattedrale) is well worth a visit. Sixteenth-century sacred vestments, Byzantine enamels and many other finely made precious items are exhibited in cases here. Perhaps the finest item, however, is the golden tiara decorated with pearls and precious gems, which once belonged to Constance of Aragon. Although originally placed in her sarcophagus with other jewels, it was later retrieved and put on display for all to admire its magnificence and beauty.

THE ARCHBISHOP'S PALACE

Archbishop Simone da Bologna, who was responsible for the design and construction of Piazza della Cattedrale, also initiated the building of the superb **Archbishop's Palace** facing the cathedral. Despite the radical restoration carried out during the 18th century, the main façade still maintains some original 15th-century features, such as the arms of the Beccadelli-Bologna family and the fine Catalan-Gothic style window with three lights. The second courtyard leads into the **Museo Diocesano**, an interesting museum founded in 1927 and enlarged in 1952, containing paintings and sculptures once housed in churches now destroyed or deconsecrated. There are also marble statues from the cathedral as well as capitals, friezes and bas-reliefs, all fine examples of Renaissance and Baroque art in Sicily.

A view of the Archbishop's palace showing the large Catalan-Gothic three-light window, a feature in the 18th-century façade.

QUATTRO CANTI

The heart of Baroque Palermo is formed by **Piazza Vigliena**, more often referred to locally as the **Quattro Canti** (Four Corners), built as part of the urban planning and reorganization which took place during the first decades of Spanish domination.

The square is formed by the crossing of the two main city centre streets, Corso Vittorio Emanuele (originally the Cassaro) and Via Maqueda which meet at right angles thus also creating four distinct and populous quarters. The corners of the junction were "chopped off" in a rather novel way, creating an intriguing octagonal arrangement, emphasized by the four resulting architecturally decorative façades in elegant Baroque style, designed by Giuseppe Lasso in 1609 and completed ten years later by Giuseppe De Avanzato. At street level each corner has a fountain, with a statue of one of the four seasons by Gregorio Tedeschi and Nunzio La Mattina. Above, the central sections have a niche containing a statue of a sovereign - Philip II, Philip III, Philip IV of Spain and the emperor Charles V - all sculpted by Giovanni Battista D'Aprile. In the upper part are marble figures of four guardian saints of the city - Agatha, Christina, Nymph and Oliva. With its central position and imposing and unusual structure, Piazza Vigliena has for long been the heart of Palermo's civic and social life where people meet, stroll and chat in the evening and where business is discussed and deals are made.

Statue of a saint located on the corner flanked by the church of San Giuseppe dei Teatini, and below, two of the 'four corners', the name by which Piazza Vigliena is better known.

S. GIUSEPPE DEI TEATINI

On one side of Piazza Vigliena, adjacent to the western corner, is the splendid church of **San Giuseppe dei Teatini**, the nave of which extends through to the other side of the 'corner', with an entrance on Piazza Pretoria. Built in the early 17th century and designed by Giacomo Besio, this majestic church is without doubt one of the most prestigious and sumptuous architectural achievements of the period in Palermo. The façade is, however, extremely simple and linear, as if intended to provide a radiant and orderly setting for the statue of Saint Cajetan (Gaetano), founder of the order of the Theatines, which dominates from its central niche. Also fascinating are the 18th-century dome, designed by Giuseppe Mariani, its lofty drum decorated with paired columns, the quite unmistakable roof glowing with coloured maiolica tiles, and the bell tower, designed by Paolo Amato. Work on the interior, a Latin cross with a nave and two aisles formed by marble columns, continued from the mid-17th century until the end of the 18th century, and is one of the most harmonious and richly decorated examples of Baroque splendour. The magnificent large frescoes in the nave, vault of the transept and the dome, by Filippo Tancredi, Guglielmo Borremans and Giuseppe Velasquez, have stucco frames by Paolo Corso and Giuseppe Serpotta. Although severely damaged during the Second World War, they have been most carefully and skilfully restored. Also worthy of note is the interesting crypt, which is, in fact, the entire body of an earlier church, the Madonna della Provvidenza, preserved by being incorporated into the new religious building.

The interior of San Giuseppe dei Teatini, and above, the 18th-century dome.

PIAZZA PRETORIA

Behind Piazza Vigliena is one of the oldest and lovliest squares in Palermo, **Piazza Pretoria**, named in 1463 after the Palazzo Pretorio, once the seat of the local Senate and now the city hall, which stands on the south side close to Piazza Bellini.

Surrounded by buildings of great architectural prestige, such as the two churches of San Giuseppe dei Teatini and Santa Caterina opposite each other, the present arrangement of the square dates from the 16th century when the entire area was razed to the ground and reorganized in 1574 to accommodate the immense fountain which still occupies most of the square. Made between 1554 and 1555 by the Florentine Mannerist sculptor and architect, Francesco Camilliani for the luxurious Tuscan residence of the viceroy don Pedro de Toledo, it was later sold to the city of Palermo by his son for the considerable sum of 30,000 scudi. In order to facilitate the rather difficult task of moving the fountain, it was dismantled into 644 pieces and patiently rebuilt directly in the square under the guidance of the sculptor's son, Camillo Camilliani. A huge and theatrical monument, the structure consists of a sequence of variously-sized basins, embellished with elegant marble decorations, allegorical figures alternating with gods, and mythological figures with animals. The 19th-century balustrading around it is by Giovan Battista Basile.

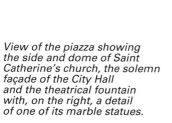

View of the piazza showing the side and dome of Saint Catherine's church, the solemn façade of the City Hall and the theatrical fountain with, on the right, a detail of one of its marble statues.

Another of the statues decorating the fountain in Piazza Pretorio, and below, the façade of the City Hall and niche containing a statue of Saint Rosalia.

CITY HALL

Built as the magistrates' courts in the 15th century, the building which now houses the city council underwent various successive and radical changes altering both its appearance and the internal structure. From Palazzo Pretorio its name changed to Palazzo Senatorio, though it is now referred to as Palazzo delle Aquile (Eagles) in honour of the relief eagle which guards the doorway. A statue of Saint Rosalia (Carlo D'Aprile, 17th century) stands atop this simple, harmonious and rather geometrically designed façade, enlivened by the attractive entrance and the many celebratory plaques recording important historical events. The city hall (Municipio) also houses many valuable works of art.

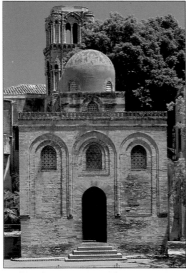

The church of San Cataldo beside Santa Maria dell'Ammiraglio, its original façade and a view of the tranquil interior.

S. CATALDO

The church of **San Cataldo**, in the centre of the city, is an elegant rectangular building with deep, blind arches on the exterior containing small, curved windows in the upper section. Commissioned in the 12th century by Admiral Majone of Bari and surmounted by three small red domes, the church is an interesting example of Norman architecture. Restoration work carried out in the 19th century removed the arbitrary modifications and additions which had been made over several centuries, revealing the original architectural simplicity of the building. The rectangular interior has a nave and two aisles and appears rather austere, the bare walls providing the backdrop for six columns, each of different origin, supporting oriental-style arches. The floor has a magnificent mosaic decoration and, like the main altar, is one of the original elements. The three small domes visible on the exterior rise from corner niches on the interior.

S. MARIA DELL'AMMIRAGLIO (THE MARTORANA)

Beside San Cataldo is the church of **Santa Maria dell'Ammiraglio** which derives its name from George of Antioch, Roger II's Admiral, who commissioned it in 1143. In 1436, by order of Alphonse of Aragon, the church passed to the convent founded in 1194 by Eloisa Martorana, thus giving it the alternative name of the **church of the Martorana**. Little remains of the original Romanesque building after the numerous alterations which have been made over the centuries.

The belltower, which originally stood flush to the façade, is highly decorated with four orders of arches and loggias lightened by mullions, small columns and inlay work. The original plan was in the form of a Greek cross, though this was lengthened and widened at the end of the 16th century, leading to the addition of a new façade on what was, in fact, the side of the building, a dome and a most Baroque main altar, all of which contribute to the eclectic charm of the entire building. In the 17th century a frescoed chapel replaced the apse of the church and a century later the structure was seriously damaged by a violent earthquake. The interior has a nave and two aisles and the upper section of the walls is completely decorated with splendid mosaics, all of which are original and among the oldest in the island of Sicily. Probably the work of Byzantine craftsmen during the mid-12th century, the mosaics illustrate scenes from the Old and New Testaments, figures of Apostles, Evangelists and Prophets, the traditional image of Christ Blessing, dominating the centre of the dome, as well as a portrait of Roger II receiving his crown from Christ and, on the north side of the nave, George of Antioch worshipping the Virgin Mary. The frescoes in the central section of the building and the presbytery, some attributed to Guglielmo Borremans, date from the 17th and 18th century alterations. The church became a cathedral of the diocese of Piana degli Albanesi in 1937 and is therefore now dedicated to the Greek-Byzantine cult.

The baroque façade of the Martorana superimposed on one side of the original Romanesque building of which the bell tower still survives.

A detail of the mosaics inside the arches, showing the Nativity.

CHIESA DEL GESÙ

The Jesuits first arrived in Sicily around 1549 and fifteen years later, having firmly established their power in the island, they began to build their first church in the centre of Palermo where a monastery had existed since the 9th century. Once an area of rocky ravines, it was traditionally popular with religious hermits, and still today there are some interesting early Christian catacombs nearby. In fact, at least five earlier churches had existed here before the Jesuits began work on the church we see today. The new building was also later enlarged by the addition of a series of side chapels and a dome, becoming one of the most interesting examples of Sicilian Baroque art though it still also maintains elements of the late Renaissance. The Latin cross interior with a nave and two aisles is extraordinarily rich with an unusually opulent decoration of marble, plasterwork and inlay, all of which are quite striking for their marked elegance. Work on the decorative arrangement was overseen by the Jesuits themselves, such as Angelo Italia da Licata, and veritable armies of craftsmen contributed to the design over at least two centuries. The frescoes on the ceiling of the central nave and presbytery are 18th-century. The chapel dedicated to Saint Anna in the left nave, is entirely decorated with magnificent marble. However, much of the church

The elegant façade of the Chiesa del Gesù, one of the most important examples of baroque architecture in Sicily, and above, the dome viewed from below.

*Details of the superb decoration of the church: below,
the magnificent altar, and above, an example of the expressive
vigour of the stucco work.*

has been modified in the course of time and it has not always been possible to respect the original structure. Serious damage caused by bombing in 1943 completely destroyed some of the frescoes (only those by Filippo Randazzo in the nave and in the vault of the presbytery survived) and these were replaced between 1954 and 1955 with paintings by Federico Spoltore.

On the right of the church is the west façade of the **Casa Professa** with an interesting doorway dated 1685 and a delightful 18th-century cloister. In the cloister is the entrance to the **city library**, housed in this most suitable of locations since 1775, fifteen years after its creation and eight years after the Jesuits were exiled from the territories of the Bourbons and consequently from their church in Palermo.

IL TEATRO MASSIMO

Details of the pediment
and capitals that decorate
the neo-classical façade of the
Teatro Massimo, seen below.

One of the largest and most prestigious theatres in Europe, the **Teatro Massimo** is most renowned for its opera performances. Designed by Giovan Battista Basile, work was begun in 1875 and completed by his son Ernesto in 1897. In order to provide a suitable setting for the new theatre, many Baroque buildings in the area were demolished to create the present-day Piazza Giuseppe Verdi. The theatre is quite majestic, with a surface area of almost 8,000 square metres and a magnificent Neoclassic façade. A wide stairway flanked by two bronze lions bearing the figures of Tragedy and Opera lead to the pronaos with six columns supporting a large pediment. On either side demi-columns and pilasters flank the numerous windows which enhance the building. The attractive interior is richly ornamented and boasts an incredible five tiers of boxes.

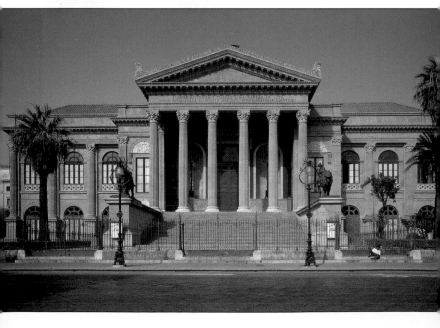

TEATRO POLITEAMA GARIBALDI

Built between 1867 and 1874 to the design and under the supervision of Giuseppe Damiani Almeyda, the **Teatro Politeama Garibaldi** dominates Piazza Ruggero Settimo with its imposing and elaborate circular structure and vivacious colours clearly intended to recall the classic example of Pompeii. The majestic entrance is similar to a triumphal arch and is crowned with a large bas-relief by Benedetto Civiletti and a group of bronze sculptures centred

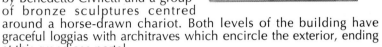

around a horse-drawn chariot. Both levels of the building have graceful loggias with architraves which encircle the exterior, ending at this grandiose portal.

Detail of the bronze chariot above the entrance to the Teatro Politeama and part of the bas relief decorating the triumphal arch which forms the impressive entrance to the theatre.

THE GALLERY OF MODERN ART

Since 1910 the top floor of the Politeama Theatre has housed the **Empedocle Restivo Gallery of Modern Art**, a prestigious collection of 235 19th- and 20th-century Italian, and especially Sicilian, works of art. It naturally complements the Regional Gallery in Palazzo Abatellis where works dated up to the late 18th century are displayed. Works exhibited in the Politeama Gallery include sculptures by Benedetto Civiletti and Ettore Ximenes and paintings by Carlo Carrà, Renato Guttuso, Gino Severini, Mario Sironi, Remo Brindisi, Domenico Purificato and Fausto Pirandello.

POLITEAMA

The open space in front of the Politeama Theatre, generally referred to simply as the Politeama, is in fact composed of two separate areas - Piazza Castelnuovo and **Piazza Ruggero Settimo**. In the latter square stands the attractive monument built in 1865 to honour the head of the provisional Sicilian government of 1848 and designed by Benedetto De Lisi Junior. At the corner of Via Ruggero Settimo is the elegant Ribaudo Cloister by Ernesto Basile (1916).

TEATRO BIONDO

In Via Roma is a church dedicated to Saint Anthony Abbot and immediately opposite this, beside the elegant Neoclassic façade of Palazzo Arezzo, stands the grandiose **Teatro Biondo**, the city's foremost prose theatre. Built in 1903 by Nicolò Mineo, the structure has a series of large windows and a rather sombre and monumental pediment.

The harmonious façade of the Teatro Biondo, and above, the entrance to the Gallery of Modern Art.

S. DOMENICO

Built in 1640 on the site of a 14th-century church which had been enlarged in 1458, the church of Saint Dominic is an attractive example of Baroque architecture. Designed by Andrea Cirrincione, the new building was not completed until 1726 when the monumental façade was added, two years after the creation of the piazza in front by demolishing houses which had, until then, suffocated the area. The church interior houses many tombs and cenotaphs of famous Sicilians, including Francesco Crispi.

A view of Piazza Castelnuovo and the façade of San Domenico.

SANTA CITA

This historic church, originally dedicated to Saint Mamiliano, was built in 1369 with a Latin cross plan. It later became the church of **Santa Cita**, though sometimes referred to as Santa Zita, and was much altered at the end of the 16th century, while the façade was not completed until the second half of the 18th century. Seriously damaged by bombing during the Second World War, the church has been carefully restored and today houses several important works of art. The adjoining **oratory** of Santa Cita is an exquisite little building, with an interior completely decorated with artistic stucco work carried out between 1688 and 1718 by one of the greatest masters of the art, Giacomo Serpotta. Allegorical scenes alternate with more traditional images of the Mysteries of the Rosary, all entirely surrounded by playful putti. At the entrance, however, is a more sombre Battle of Lepanto, while the wooden benches around the walls are magnificently inlaid with mother-of-pearl.

The magnificent interior of the Santa Cita Oratorio and the fine stuccowork which decorates the walls and frames the image of the Battle of Lepanto above the entrance (below).

IL MUSEO ARCHEOLOGICO REGIONALE

The **Archaeological Museum** is housed in a 17th-century building, originally the monastery of the Padri Filippini dell'Olivella, which was severely damaged by bombing during the Second World War and is now fully restored. One of the most important of its kind in Italy, the museum's extensive collection provides a comprehensive panorama of the various civilizations which inhabited Sicily from the Phoenicians to the Carthaginians, from the Greeks to the Romans, in all their various artistic forms. Founded at the beginning of the 19th century as a university museum, it was transferred to its present location, where it occupies three floors, in 1866.

On the ground floor the two cloisters and the adjacent rooms house many items recovered from the sea bed, sculptures in both classical and oriental style, as well as items from Tindari, Imera and Agrigento. The larger hall contains artefacts and remains from Selinunte, including numerous pairs of stele, a magnificent collection of metopes from the grand temples of the city once decorated with wonderful sculptures and bas-reliefs, and the renowned Selinunte Ephebus, a bronze statue dating from the 5th century B.C. Originating entirely from Chiusi and also housed in a large area on the ground floor, the interesting Etruscan collection contains funerary urns, sarcophagi, clay vessels and tombstones, all dating from the 7th to the 1st century B.C.

Displayed in the first floor gallery are various materials found throughout the island, from Marsala to Segesta, from Termini Imerese to Solunto. Alongside lanterns, painted terracotta, and items found in the necropoli around Palermo, are large and small Greek, Etruscan and Roman bronzes such as the famous Syracuse Ram (3rd century B.C.) and Hercules subduing a stag from Pompeii. Other rooms contain fragments from the Parthenon as well as collections of jewellery and coins. There are some outstanding items in the numismatic collection such as the Syracuse decadramus and the famous coin of the legend of the Siceliotes.

On the second floor are the collections of prehistoric, paleolithic and neolithic remains belonging to the Bronze, Copper and Iron

Above, a fine example of painted ceramic, and in the centre, a 6th-century B.C. Etruscan architectural ornament. Left, the Syracuse Ram, a powerfully realistic bronze sculpture.

This monumental metope from one of the temples of Selinunte, sculpted with beautiful bas-reliefs of mythological scenes, represents the degree of sophistication Sicilian art had achieved. Left, the lid of a canopic jar from Chiusi (Etruscan art, 6th century B.C.).

Ages. These include items ranging from utensils to weapons, from early rudimental ornaments to important Greek and Italic ceramics, displayed in separate rooms, as well as mosaics and frescoes of the Roman period. The Greek ceramics are of particular importance with outstandingly elegant and sophisticated craters decorated with wonderful mythological scenes: the ascent of Hercules to Olympus on the vase from Gela, the departure of Triptolemus in a winged chariot on a vase found at Agrigento. Another most beautiful item from Gela is the 5th-century B.C. crater of the Amazons. Also fascinating are the large

mosaics, such as the highly expressive Orpheus, surrounded by the enchanted wild beasts. The room containing the Roman sculptures is of particular importance, housing numerous statues, busts and portraits, as well as sarcophagi of important personages, including some emperors, discovered in various parts of Sicily.

Left, a copy of the famous Laocoon *in the Vatican Museum. Above, one of the fine lions' heads that decorate the eaves on the Temple of Victory at Imera (5th century B.C.).*

41

LA VUCCIRIA

The lively and characteristic **Vucciria market** in Piazza della Concordia is one of the most spontaneous features of everyday life in the city of Palermo, providing a genuine impression of the traditions and customs of Sicily. Amidst the stalls of lemons, oranges and fresh swordfish and the intense colours and smells, the amazing warmth of the island's inhabitants is most vibrantly evident. The unique characters of the market are the real celebrities of the city, from the knife grinder, proud of being one of the few remaining in Palermo, to Vincenzo, a fruit and vegetable stall-holder, from Antonio who sells herbs and spices, to Salvatore who runs a fish stall, famous for the vast variety on offer. At the market, even shopping becomes a pleasant and entertaining pastime, as well as an interesting way of getting to know the city.

Views of the picturesque Vucciria market: a shop selling spices, olives and chilies, a fruit and vegetable stall and a fishmonger.

Another view of this
most popular market
where all kinds of food
are sold, from fruit
to new-baked bread,
from local vegetables
to freshly caught fish,
especially tuna
and swordfish.

43

S. FRANCESCO D'ASSISI

Not far from Corso Vittorio Emanuele, in the centre of Palermo's old town, once a thriving area inhabited by rich merchants, the first **church** of the mendicant order of Saint Francis of Assisi was built. Its history is long and troubled: built between 1255 and 1277 on a site where there had previously been two other churches, it was considerably altered during the 15th century when the side chapels were made, in 1533 when the cross vaults were added, in 1589 when the presbytery was lengthened and widened, in 1723 when the attractive stucco decoration was added by Giacomo Serpotta providing a suitable complement to the frescoes completed during the previous century, in 1823 when repairs were required following a violent earthquake and the opportunity was taken to renovate the interior in the Neoclassic style so popular at the time. Finally, when the church suffered devasting damage during the bombing of 1943, radical renovation was carried out, returning the church to its original 13th-century appearance. This is also evident on the exterior of the building where some elements of the early structure have survived along the right side and at the crossing of the apses. Today the façade, sensitively restored at the end of the 19th century, still has the fine Gothic doorway, made in the early 14th century and crowned by an attractive aedicule and large rose-window. The two side doors, however, are in more sombre Renaissance style and probably date from the second half of the 16th century. The interior, with a nave and two aisles, is enhanced by wide and lofty arches and Gothic and Renaissance chapels in the side aisles which are separated from the nave by two rows of round columns. The church also contains interesting works of art such as the sculptures by Antonio and Giacomo Gagini and Francesco Laurana, and the splendid inlayed wooden choir stalls dating from the 16th century. The allegorical statues decorating the nave are exceptionally fine works made by Giacomo Serpotta in 1723. The church also has an important Treasury with numerous paintings and religious furnishings which date from the 15th to the 19th century.

The façade of San Francesco d'Assisi, and above, the rose-window.

CHIESA DELLA MAGIONE

A fine and venerable example of Norman architecture, the **church of the Magione** was founded by Matteo d'Ajello in 1191 for the Cistercian monks, though in 1197 it was given by emperor Henry VI to the Teutonic Order with whom it remained until the end of the 15th century. The church still maintains the austere severity of its original appearance as a result of the massive task of restoration carried out after bomb damage caused during the Second World War. All structural additions and alterations made to the church over the centuries were removed, and as a result the façade has a delightful series of double-linteled arches reflecting the subtle, interlinking arches which highlight the tripartite structure of the apse. The interior has a nave and two aisles divided by marble columns supporting Gothic arches while the

The severely linear façade of the Magione church and a view of the unusually simple, unadorned interior.

floor, partially reconstructed, still contains the tombstones of some Teutonic knights.

The remains of the 12th-century cloisters on the left of the church are most interesting; the side which has been restored has small paired columns crowned by delicate capitals and supporting pointed arches, also with double lintels, elements which seem to support the theory that the cloister was built before that of Monreale and by the same craftsmen.

PUPPETS AND BALLAD SINGERS

W ithout doubt one of the most renowned and unique features of Sicilian folklore are the marionettes, puppets which derive from the Norman-Arabian courtly tradition and from the French Paladins, and which for centuries have been the most important feature of a fascinating and highly popular form of entertainment. It is not surprising therefore that Palermo should boast an **International Puppet Museum** (Museo Internazionale delle Marionette), in Via Butera, where the collection contains not only the traditional puppets of Palermo and Trapani, and the classic Neapolitan marionettes, but also items from all over the world and some fine elaborate scenery.

The city also has a **Puppet Theatre** (Teatro dell'Opera dei Pupi) which keeps this ancient tradition alive. This same cultural institution also preserves and fosters the art of the **ballad singers** who relate the acts of heroes and historic events, illustrated by brightly coloured paintings whose simplicity and naivety are quite charming. Especially appealing, although not very old as it was made in the 1960's, is the

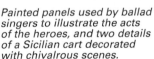

Painted panels used by ballad singers to illustrate the acts of the heroes, and two details of a Sicilian cart decorated with chivalrous scenes.

On the left, some of the famous Sicilian puppets.

ballad illustrated by the 'Figli d'Arte Cuticchio', patiently restored by Mimmo Cuticchio who is descended from a long line of puppeteers.
Scenes from the days of chivalry also decorate the traditional Sicilian carts which can still be seen in the streets of Palermo. A particularly interesting example, belonging to the collection of Franco Bertolino, has a highly colourful and animated battle scene painted on the back.

View of La Cala, a natural inlet that formed the earliest port of Palermo, today used only by leisure craft.

LA CALA

The sheltered and welcoming gulf of Palermo has always been an important base for the commercial and maritime routes which worked the Mediterranean. The city gained considerable and lasting benefits from its position and despite numerous alterations and the inevitable enlargement of the port, the original landing point, until the 16th century the city's only harbour, is still used by leisure craft. Known as **La Cala**, this small natural bay was once much deeper than now and it was here that the original nucleus of the ancient settlement came into being.

THE PORT

Towards the mid 16th century, as the volume of traffic calling at Palermo increased, the city began to outgrow the small natural harbour at La Cala. A dock was therefore built further to the north in 1567, enclosed by an extensive jetty, one of the most innovative and impressive feats of engineering of the day. However, with the passing of time the new **port** continued to grow and develop as large shipyards were built behind the docks, warehouses and storage for goods were installed and a large dry-dock was added, making Palermo the most important harbour of the entire island. During the early years of the 20th century, Palermo was the main point of departure for the numerous emigrants who left for America. The port was later partially destroyed by bombing during the Second World War and was subsequently rebuilt with more modern infrastructures, including the construction of the new offshore barrier to protect the three existing docks in 1973. Standing at the entrance to the harbour area is a bronze statue of a woman holding a laurel branch on high, welcoming all those who arrive in Palermo by sea. This elegant, flowing figure was made by Nino Geraci, a local sculptor.

The statue that stands at the entrance to the port of Palermo, and the deck of a naval ship.

PIAZZA MARINA

In 1863 G. B. F. Basile designed **Piazza Marina**, thus creating the present picturesque square. The attractive layout he developed resolved the problem of the large, flattened area which had come into being as the result of centuries of infilling in La Cala inlet. To improve the appearance of the area, the Garibaldi Gardens were made, a park filled with exotic plants and surrounded by an impressive enclosure. Facing onto the square are the church of Santa Maria dei Miracoli and the grandly austere Palazzo Denti Fatta and Palazzo Notarbartolo Greco.

S. MARIA DELLA CATENA

The interior of Santa Maria della Catena showing the series of Renaissance columns, and below, the façade.

Adjacent to La Cala is the church of **Santa Maria della Catena**, named after the chain (catena) which for centuries was used to close the old port of the city. Standing above a wide flight of steps is an elegant portico with three doorways each decorated with a bas relief. The church is remarkable for the Catalan-Gothic style of architecture which, however, combines quite harmoniously with typically Renaissance elements. Built in the 16th century, the interior has a spacious nave and two aisles leading to the raised presbytery and three apses.

PALAZZO CHIARAMONTE

Also known as "Steri" from the corruption of the Latin "hosterium" (fortified building) the imposing square structure of **Palazzo Chiaramonte**, planned around a central atrium, was built in the 14th century by the most powerful feudal family of Sicily at the time. With the extinction of the Chiaramonte line their palace became first the residence of the viceroys, and from 1601 the court of the Holy Office. From 1799 to 1960 it housed the Law Courts and is at present the seat of the Rectorate.

PALAZZO ABATELLIS

Built towards the end of the 15th century for Francesco Abatellis, prefect of Palermo, **Palazzo Abatellis**, is an imposing yet elegant building designed by Matteo Carnelivari in Catalan-Gothic style with clear Renaissance influences.
Following the damage caused by bombing during the Second

A view of the 14th-century Palazzo Chiaramonte.

Below left, the Triumph of Death *housed in the palazzo, and on the right the courtyard of Palazzo Abatellis where an important art collection is housed.*

World War, the building was entirely restored and altered to house the **Regional Gallery of Sicily** (Galleria Regionale della Sicilia), an important collection of paintings and sculptures dating from the Middle Ages to the end of the 18th century.
The museum is housed on two floors and begins with sculptures from the pre-Romanesque period to the 16th century, exhibited in the entrance hall and courtyard. Among the many magnificent and unique works of art are: the Triumph of Death, a 15th-century fresco representing a fascinating allegory of death, formerly in Palazzo Sclafani; a bust of Eleanor of Aragon, a Renaissance sculpture by Francesco Laurana (1471); the Malvagna Tryptych by the Flemish

artist, Jan Gossaert, dated 1510;
and, most famous of all, the
lovely Annunziata by Antonello
da Messina.

A bust of Eleanor of Aragon
by Laurana, the Annunciation
*by Antonello da Messina
and one of the spacious rooms
in the gallery.*

S. MARIA DEGLI ANGELI (LA GANCIA)

Santa Maria degli Angeli was built in the 16th-century over an earlier church dedicated to Saint Jerome. The sombre façade of plain square blocks is enhanced by a large Gothic entrance crowned by a bas-relief. The large nave is lit from a series of windows at roof level and was substantially altered in the 17th century to create the tranquil and harmonious interior seen today. One of the most important features of the church is the organ located above the entrance; made by Raffaele La Valle in 1620 it is now the oldest in Palermo. The fine stucco work in the presbytery is by Giacomo Serpotta and the lovely decorations and reliefs are by Antonello Gagini and his workshop.

The interior of the church of Santa Maria degli Angeli, and above, the 17th-century organ located above the entrance.

S. TERESA ALLA KALSA

Close to Palazzo Abatellis is one of the oldest parts of Palermo, the **Kalsa**, a name derived from the Arab term meaning "chosen". It was in this area that the emir chose to build his residence and today the magnificent church of **Santa Teresa**, one of the finest examples of Sicilian Baroque, stands here, its attractive façade overlooking Piazza della Kalsa. Designed by Giacomo Amato and built between 1686 and 1706, the church has a single, bright and airy nave decorated with delightful stucco work made in the early 18th century by Giuseppe and Procopio Serpotta.

A detail of the Holy Family that decorates the entrance to Santa Teresa alla Kalsa, one of the statues in a niche flanking the doorway, and the baroque façade of the church.

The remains of the church of Santa Maria dello Spasimo.

S. MARIA DELLO SPASIMO

Near to the Kalsa and the church of Santa Teresa, are the ruins of **Santa Maria dello Spasimo**, still evocative despite the deterioration caused by the passing of time. Built in 1506, the church became a hospice for the poor, the sick and pilgrims. The painting, now in the Prado Museum in Madrid, entitled Jesus Falling under the Cross, better known as Lo Spasimo di Sicilia was executed by Raphael for the church which eventually took its name from this great work. The original majesty of the building is still quite evident in these evocative ruins which have now been sensitively adapted to house exhibitions and performances. Despite, or perhaps as a result of, the obvious deterioration of the entire building, much of which now lacks a roof, the setting is highly romantic, forming a kind of delightful open-air theatre.

The elegant exedrae in the formal gardens of Villa Giulia and the unusual statue in the fountain in the centre.

VILLA GIULIA

Near to the seafront is a magnificent Italianate garden based on a design of 1778 by Nicolò Palma, extended and enlarged in 1866, with a square, geometrically arranged layout of concentric radial sections. The first public garden in Palermo, it was named **Villa Giulia** after Giulia Guevara, wife of the Spanish viceroy, and is noted for the elegant Neoclassic exedra, semicircular structures with recesses, which stand around the fountain in the centre of the gardens. Along the avenues are busts of famous personages of the city.

THE BOTANICAL GARDENS

A view of the Botanical Gardens.

Beside the Villa Giulia gardens, and appearing to be a natural extension of them, are the Botanical Gardens created by Ferdinand III in 1785. Extending around the Neoclassical Gymnasium designed by Leone de Fourny, now the Herbarium, the **gardens** cover an area of almost ten hectares with paths winding around the Calidarium and the Tepidarium, designed by Venanzio Marvuglia (1789). Divided into four distinct botanical sections are the most varied examples of flowers, plants and trees from all over the world, some centuries old, while others have grown to immense size. Palermo's botanical garden is one of the most splendid and interesting not only in Europe, but in the world.

S. GIOVANNI
DEI LEBBROSI

One of the most simple and archaic buildings of Norman Palermo is **San Giovanni dei Lebbrosi**, founded in 1070 by Roger I, though only completed a century later. Probably by then the church had also built the hospital for lepers, giving it the name by which it is still known. Set amidst a pretty palm grove, it has a small entrance and a bell-tower which was added to the main façade at a later date. Recent restoration has removed the Baroque alterations made to the church, revealing the original, plain and unadorned interior with a nave and two aisles defined by pilasters supporting Gothic arches.

The interior of the church restored to its original sobriety.

The church of San Giovanni dei Lebbrosi showing the belltower added at a later date, and the shady palms and trees surrounding it.

PONTE DELL'AMMIRAGLIO

The **Admiral's Bridge** with its seven arches, all of different heights, still stands where once the river Oreto flowed before being deviated. Like the church of the Martorana, it was built in the 12th century by George of Antioch, Roger II's admiral. The use of undressed stone and the double lintels which define the characteristic ogival arches are typically Norman architectural features. Progressive infilling below the bridge has partially obstructed the arches, diminishing the emphatic pyramidal form the bridge once had. On arriving in Sicily in May 1860, Garibaldi's troops engaged in their first battle with the Bourbon forces near the Admiral's Bridge.

LA CUBA AND LA CUBOLA

Of all the Norman buildings in the city, **La Cuba** is the most typical example of Eastern architecture. Rectangular in shape with blind arcading around each side, small windows, niches and retaining walls reinforced by projections, it became a barracks for cavalry troops under the Bourbons. Built by William II in 1180 in the centre of a luxuriant royal park and surrounded by an artificial lake, its original function was, however, that of a leisure pavilion. Probably fascinated by its beauty and

Two views of the Ponte dell'Ammiraglio now partially submerged and contrasting oddly with the modern urban surroundings.

renown, Boccaccio set one of the tales from the Decameron here. La Cuba later had various private owners and during the 16th century became a hospital for those suffering from contagious diseases.

Also situated in the park and commissioned by William II at the end of the 12th century is the smaller, but equally imposing **Cubola**, made of heavily rusticated stone, with lofty arches and a semicircular red dome. The name derives from the cube shape of the building but, although slightly less sophisticated, its Norman style saves it from ignominy compared to the more 'noble' Cuba and Zisa.

The Cubola, topped by a red hemispherical dome, and above, a model showing the elegant Cuba which originally stood reflected in a lake.

LA ZISA

Quite close to La Cuba and originally also in the grounds of the royal park, is **La Zisa**, another superb example of Norman architecture in the Eastern style with mighty walls flanked by square towers and enhanced by blind arches and slender windows. It was commissioned in the 12th century by William I as a summer house and was built on the edge of a lake, in what was probably the centre of the Conca d'Oro, at the time an area of great beauty and ideal for the rest and recreation of the ruling family. Completed by William II, La Zisa, a name derived from the Arab "aziz" meaning "splendid", was designed with both private and public rooms. The private rooms were located in the elegant royal appartments on the upper floors, while the public rooms were entered through a large hall and were arranged around the immense Sala della Fontana (Hall of the Fountain). The façades are delicately decorated with fine detail, however, the elegant internal arrangement was considerably altered by various owners subsequent to the Norman dynasty, and the entire building was finally abandoned. This unusual structure has recently been bought by the Region of Sicily and should at last enjoy a new lease of life, fully restored to its original splendour.

The main façade of the Ziza, and above, a detail of the coat of arms over the entrance.

The Capuchin monastery, and below, part of the catacombs.

CONVENTO DEI CAPPUCCINI

An important church had stood on this site since Norman times and in 1621 the **Capuchin church** and **monastery** were built here. Despite the alterations made in 1934, important 18th-century works still remain such as the wooden altar, imposing funerary monuments by Ignazio Marabitti and a fine wooden Crucifix dating from the late Middle Ages.

The building is best known, however, for the catacombs, chosen by many of the city's most famous personages as their final resting place in the period from the early 17th century until 1881. The passageways in the catacombes are reserved for, respectively, ecclesiastics, women and the 'professional classes', and contain thousands of remains, mainly skeletons, though some bodies are mummified or embalmed; all are perfectly dressed, standing, sitting, or lying in coffins. Macabre, yet at the same time awesome, this most unusual sight represents the importance of a custom that was deeply rooted in the traditions of Palermo's wealthy society. The poet Ippolito Pindemonte was deeply affected by the images and atmosphere of the catacombes, which inspired some of the verses in his Sepolcri (Sepulchres).

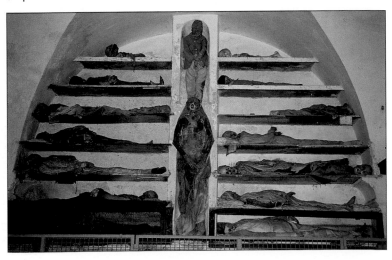

S. MARIA DELLA PIETÀ

The magnificent church of **Santa Maria della Pietà** was built between 1678 and 1684 by Giacomo Amato, who drew much of his inspiration from the early Roman Baroque style as is evident from the architecturally ornate, yet sophisticated, façade dominating Via Torremuzza. Consisting of two orders of fine columns, and ornamented with a range of differing decorative elements (niches, sculptures, oculi and an elaborate rose-window) it represents all the most unusual features of typically Baroque opulence. The sumptuous yet harmonious interior is also a fine example of the period. The nave is superbly decorated with artistic stucco work by Giuseppe and Procopio Serpotta, dating from the early 18th century. The large frescoes which decorate the nave, the presbytery and the area below the choir, are of great beauty adding to the undeniable charm of the rich decoration that adorns and enhances every corner of the church.

Two statues decorating the façade of the magnificent baroque church, Santa Maria della Pietà; below left, the elaborate inner façade.

The vaulted ceiling of the nave showing the wealth of frescoes, and the interior of the church richly decorated with paintings and stuccowork.

Some of the many rare and ancient trees in the Favorita Park.

THE FAVORITA PARK

Lying between Palermo and Mondello, at the foot of Monte Pellegrino, is the extensive **Favorita Park**, created in 1799 by king Ferdinand III of Bourbon, who had been obliged to transfer his residence to Palermo following the entry of Napoleon's troops to Naples. The king intended the park to be used as a large fishing and hunting reserve, as well as for argricultural experimentation, one of his greatest interests.

Today, the entrance to the park is from the Porta Leoni, and the four hundred hectares are crossed by two main avenues, the Diana Avenue and the Hercules Avenue, the latter ending at the fountain of the same name, decorated with a copy of the Farnese Hercules now housed in the National Museum of Naples. New structures and sports facilites have also recently been introduced to improve the Favorita Park.

The unusual mixture of styles of the remarkable Chinese Pavilion give it a particularly bizarre appearance; below, a bust of Giuseppe Pitré who founded the ethnographical museum named after him.

THE CHINESE PAVILION

Inside the Favorita Park is the **Chinese Pavilion** (Palazzina Cinese), a highly unusual mixture of different styles designed and built in 1799 by Venanzio Marvuglia for king Ferdinand III of Bourbon. Indeed, the king and his wife, Marie Caroline, must have spent a considerable amount of time in the building during the period of Napoleonic occupation of Naples when they were forced to move to Sicily.

The 'pavilion' uninhibitedly and rather successfully combines the Neoclassic element of the columns on the upper floor and the medieval style of the Gothic arches on the ground floor, while at the same time introducing some of the more unusual architectural elements of follies and Chinese motifs so popular at the time, which gave the pavilion its name. Lord Nelson and Emma Hamilton were among the many famous guests who stayed in this original little palace.

Of particular note in this most unusual and rather exotic building, are the two small towers at the sides, with spiral staircases leading up to a terrace, a rather elegant feature designed by Giuseppe Patricolo, providing an ideal area for rest and relaxation. At present the pavilion houses a collection of prints and Chinese silks as well as a collection of 18th-century paintings.

MUSEO ETNOGRAFICO PITRÉ

The **Ethnographic Museum** developed from the unique collection of Giuseppe Pitré, an enthusiastic scholar of ethnography who studied the folklore and traditions of Sicily in general, and Palermo in particular. In 1909 the collection was moved to a building beside the Chinese

Pavilion, originally the quarters of the servants to the Bourbon household. Between 1934 and 1935 the collection was reorganized and augmented by the expert Giuseppe Cocchiara, who also updated the documentation of these important items. The museum is now one of the most important in Europe and includes reconstructions of interiors, such as the interesting 17th-century home of a middle-class family, providing fascinating insights into Sicilian life, everyday activities, the traditions of the island, and typical local crafts. All aspects of work and daily life are represented such as spinning and weaving, hunting, fishing, farming, all kinds of ceramics, from the simplest to the most elegant, from musical instruments to carriages. The magnificent traditional cribs are also exhibited and include a splendid example from Trapani made at the end of the 18th century and attributed to Giovanni Matera. There are also collections of ex-voto, of items used in magical rites such as driving out the evil eye, and a complete puppet theatre in full working order.

Several rooms in the Pitré Ethnographical Museum, and below, the main entrance.

An aerial view of the beautiful bay where the delightful small town of Mondello lies and, below a detail of the Mermaid statue decorating the fountain in the main square.

MONDELLO

About ten kilometres from Palermo, beyond the Favorita Park, is **Mondello**, a favourite resort for the residents of Palermo, in an attractive inlet with Monte Pellegrino on one side and Monte Gallo on the other. On the northern side of the bay, protected by watch towers built in the 15th century and still standing today, a small fishing community developed in times of old. Although it prospered by tuna fishing, the village was surrounded by most unhealthy marshes. Drainage and reclamation carried out in the late 19th and early 20th centuries lead to the creation of a delightful 'garden city' and radically changed the character of the area which rapidly became a refined seaside resort for the elite who built most elegant residences here at the height of the 'Belle Epoque' period. One of the finest symbols of this golden age is the unique Kursaal a mare, a grand and unusual bathing establishment which juts out over the blue sea of the bay. After the Second World War, as tourism gradually became a mass phenomenon, the elitest nature of the resort gradually diminished without, however, spoiling the great natural beauty of the area, which has always been protected by regulations

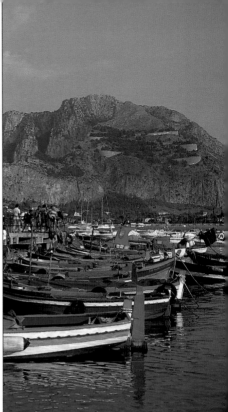

The old fishing port with its superb natural setting, and the entrance and façade of the famous bathing establishment, Kursaal a mare.

and limited planning permission for new constructions. Today Mondello is almost a suburb of Palermo, yet it is still a first class tourist area of international renown due to the excellent modern infrastructures and the magnificent natural setting. In the caves on the rocky slopes of Monte Gallo and Monte Pellegrino a further and fascinating attraction is to be found; as well as being of speleological interest, numerous Paleolithic graffiti by prehistoric man, representing animals and human figures, have been discovered in caves such as the Addaura. Various artefacts were also found here and are now in the Archaeological Museum of Palermo.

THE SAINT ROSALIA SANCTUARY

In the mid-12th century a young woman named Rosalia, traditionally believed to have belonged to the ruling Norman family and perhaps a niece of William II took refuge in a cave on Monte Pellegrino, dedicating herself to a life of prayer and penance. From the top of this rough, scaly hill, high on the western side of Palermo, one has a magnificent view over the sparkling blue of the bay. After her death around 1166, a widespread cult of enthusiastic and popular devotion developed, leading to her beatification and, shortly after, to her adoption as patron saint of the city. One of the miracles attributed to Rosalia is the ending of the dreadful plague which ravaged Palermo in the 17th century and which only ceased when the bones of the saint were discovered on 15 July 1624, after she appeared in a vision to reveal where they were buried. In recognition and thanksgiving, that same year a large **sanctuary** and convent were built on the spot where Rosalia had lived and prayed. This sombre Baroque building has since become a place of pilgrimage, and the water which drips from the walls of the cave is believed to be miraculous. The expressive statues of the saint are also objects of religious devotion: one stands in a white niche on the ochre-coloured façade, another stands in front of the sanctuary, welcoming the faithful, and yet another and more famous, is on an altar inside the cave, with a sumptuous canopy above. The marble figure of the saint is clothed in a splendid golden cape donated by Charles III of Bourbon. On 4 September every year a procession winds its way along the twisting roads which climb the slopes of Monte Pellegrino, following a route offering incomparably beautiful, panoramic views, to arrive at the sanctuary and cave and render homage to the venerated image of Palermo's patron saint.

A statue of Saint Rosalia, the castle of Utveggio and two views of the grotto where the saint withdrew to live in penitence.

Facing page, the sanctuary built high on the slopes of Monte Pellegrino.

MONREALE

Monreale lies a short distance from Palermo on the gentle slopes of Monte Caputo, looking towards the outstandingly beautiful Conca d'Oro where there was once a vast and fertile hunting reserve for the aristocratic Arabs and ruling Normans. The name itself indicates that the area once belonged entirely to the rulers of Sicily. Over the centuries, the ancient Arab village which stood high above the Oreto valley, perched on a ledge at a height of 310 metres, grew and developed around the grand cathedral and today Monreale is an attractive small town surrounded by lemon and orange groves and orchards. The town is famous for its fine wines and excellent oil as well as being the birthplace (1603) of Pietro Novelli, a renowned painter otherwise known as "Il Monrealese". Today this rather pretty centre produces a wide range of high quality crafts, including baskets, shoes and even furniture. The main economic resource of the town, however, is without doubt tourism based on the fine Romanesque and Norman art and architecture of the monuments, surrounded by a group of small, historic houses.

Aerial view of Monreale clearly showing the austerely elegant outline of the cathedral with the beautiful portico along the side, the cloister, the remaining walls of the ancient refectory and the new monastery.

The façade of the cathedral with its two square towers and the 18th-century portico.

A sculpture on the fountain in the centre of Piazza Vittorio Emanuele, which flanks the cathedral.

THE CATHEDRAL

Despite the passing of time and growth of the town, the centre of Monreale is still around the square of the cathedral - a Romanesque building, austere and linear in style. It was commissioned in 1166 by the Norman king, William II who succeeded his father, William I, when only twelve years old. Until he was of age, his mother, Margaret of Navarre, acted as regent. According to popular tradition, the church was built on the spot where, while resting during a hunting party, the Virgin appeared to the young king to show him where William I had buried his vast treasure, subsequently used to build the cathedral.

It is more probable, however, that William II was well aware of the importance and significance of the

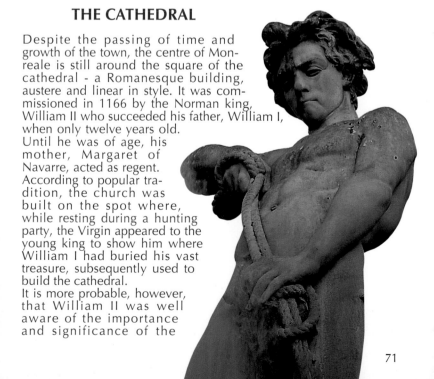

71

magnificent and grandiose monuments and works of art commissioned by his predecessor, Roger II, especially the Palatine Chapel and the cathedral of Cefalù (1130-1131), and was determined to build a cathedral which would outshine even the splendours of Palermo. Thus, in 1172, as soon as his mother's guardianship came to an end, he initiated work on this new religious complex, probably built on the site of an earlier monastery and intended to include a convent and sumptuous royal palace. Speedy progress was made and as early as 1176, one hundred Benedictine monks under the guidance of Abbot Theobald arrived from the important and powerful Abbey of the Trinity at Cava dei Tirreni. In the same year the nascent church was dedicated to the Blessed Virgin Mary and, with the approval of pope Alexander III, was granted extensive property and important privileges by the king.

In 1183 another pope, Lucius III, made the abbot of the monastery an archbishop and raised the church to the level of metropolitan cathedral. When William II died in 1189, the church of which he was so proud, a splendid combination of Byzantine, Arab and Norman architecture, was almost completely finished. The stupendous main doorway in bronze, one of the finest works of Bonanno Pisano who arrived from Pisa by sea, was already in place, as well as the equally fine side door by Barisano da Trani. The former consists of 42 bronze panels representing scenes from the Old and New Testaments with texts in the vernacular, while the latter, also with two

The exterior of the cathedral apse showing the houses closely huddled around it.

The elaborate wooden ceiling which, although almost completely remade after the disasterous fire in 1811, has a geometric design and colour scheme derived from the most widespread Arabian ornamental styles and patterns.

Following pages, a magnificent view of the inside of the nave, gleaming with mosaics and showing the small partition separating it from the stupendous transept. At the far end is the beautiful vault decorated with immense mosiac figures.

leaves, has panels with images of the Saviour and various saints.
The interior of the building still did not have the decorated pavements in the nave and in the aisles nor the marble decoration on the lower part of the walls. However, the general impression must have been quite splendid and would, no doubt, have fully satisfied William II's ideal of magnificence.
On the outside, the absence of a dome was compensated for by the presence of two rectangular towers, a typical feature of Norman architecture, though the one on the left was not entirely completed.
However, the death of William II, immediately followed by a series of complex and troubled events which soon lead to the fall of the Norman dynasty, caused work on the cathedral to come almost to a halt, while at the same time the fortunes of the adjoining Benedictine monastery also took a turn for the worse.
Consequently, despite the near completion of the building, it was not consecrated until 1267 by Bishop Rudolph of Albano, representing pope Clement IV, who dedicated it to the Blessed Virgin Mary.

William II, his parents and his brothers, Roger and Harry, were already buried there. The body of Saint Louis of France (king Louis IX), who died in Tunis, was later brought to the cathedral of Monreale, but it was decided to return his body to France and only some relics now remain here, preserved in an urn beneath the altar. At the end of the 13th century, however, the splendid cathedral was still not entirely completed. Indeed there was no sacristy until the late 15th century while the pavement of the nave and the aisles and the splendid floor of the left transept were not finished until a century later. The pavements are made of white marble from quarries in Taormina inlaid with discs of porphery and granite, and were designed by Baldassare Massa in the mid-16th century. The portico along the side was made in 1547 to a design by Gian Domenico and Fazio Gagini lending a refined Renaissance touch to the

Facing page: the Creation of Eve *from Adam's rib and* Original Sin.

Eve tempted by the serpent *which persuades her to disobey God's will.*

severity of the exterior. The Chapel of Saint Castrense dates from 1595 and the opulent Chapel of the Crucifix, a splendid example of elaborate Baroque art, a century later. The Chapel of Saint Castrense is named for Monreale's patron saint and was commissioned by archbishop Ludovico II Torres, who wished to be buried there. Destiny decreed otherwise, however, as the prelate died in 1609 in Rome where he is buried in the crypt of Saint Pancras. The chapel he had built in Monreale is elegantly Renaissance in style, discreetly decorated and crowned with a dome supported by a high drum. It contains a marble statue of the archbishop and below the marble altar, standing beneath a graceful canopy, are the relics of Saint Castrense, traditionally believed to have been given to William II by the Archbishop of Capua. The chapel of the Crucifix, glowing with various coloured marbles, was begun in 1690 by the Jesuit architect, Angelo Italia da Licata, though the original project may be attributed to the Capuchin monk Giovanni da Monreale. It was consecrated on 14 September 1692 by Giovanni Roano, the Spanish archbishop who commissioned it. The magnificent cathedral Treasury is now housed in this chapel.

In the meantime, the building had begun to show the first signs of deterioration, leading to successive phases of repair and restoration. In particular, work was carried out on the ceiling and the mosaics, while the choir was completely rebuilt, the altars replaced and a small crenellated section was added to the tower on the left of the façade, to house the bells. Built around an elegant cloister, the monastery had also been considerably altered when part of it was converted into the archbishop's residence during the 16th century. The royal palace had been turned into a seminary in 1589.

On 24 December 1770 the original portico on the façade, a structure with four marble columns and Corinthian capitals supporting three ogival arches, entirely collapsed, despite having been frequently restored. It was replaced by the present portico, designed by Antonio Romano and made by Ignazio Marabitti, a sculptor from Palermo. Although a light, elegant structure, it looks rather uncomfortable compared to the interwoven arches of limestone and lava framing the window with pointed arches on the upper part of the façade, reflecting the decoration of the apse inside.

In 1807 the tower on the right was struck by lightning and the pinnacle crowning it was destroyed, never to be replaced.

A few years later, on 11 November 1811, a disastrous fire, probably caused by a careless choir boy, ruined much of the church, destroying the ceiling, the organs, the choir and seriously damaging the sepulchres and mosaics. So devastating was the image of the dread-

ful damage caused, that it was decided to begin the task of reconstruction immediately, but given the extent of the work involved, it inevitably took many years to complete. In 1926 the cathedral was raised to the level of 'minor basilica' and thanks to continual restoration and conservation, the building is once more seen in its original splendour.

The interior has a nave and two aisles ending in three apses and the church's greatest splendour and most renowned feature is seen here. The quite stupendous, glowing cycles of **mosaics** are composed of 130 panels, surrounded by a myriad of figures, and almost entirely cover the walls of the building, some 10,000 square metres in all, forming one of the largest areas of mosaic in the world. William II himself almost certainly participated in the choice of subjects and the overall iconographic plan, with the expert advice of the monks, especially the English archdeacon, Walter of the Mill (Gualtiero Offamilio) and the vice-chancellor, Matteo d'Ajello. On the whole, the arrangement of the subjects portrayed in the mosaics reflects the heirarchy normally found in Byzantine art; consequently the areas of

Facing page: Noah releases the animals after the flood, *the* Drunkeness of Noah *and the* Building of the Tower of Babel.

Below, The Healing of the Leper.

The Sacrifice of Isaac *and the* Transfiguration.

Facing page: Christ walks on the water and saves Peter,
the Raising of the daughter of Jairus *and* Christ chases
the money lenders from the temple.

the church of greater symbolic importance contain the figures and events of greatest significance in Christian doctrine. In the central apse, for example, towering over the image of the Blessed Virgin, is the radiant figure of Christ as Pantocrator, surrounded by heavenly bodies such as the Archangels (with two wings), the Cherubim and Seraphim (with six wings) and Tetramorphs (with four heads), as well as Prophets, Apostles, Bishops and Saints, the followers of Christ in the world. The two side apses are dedicated to the apostles, Peter and Paul and illustrate their stories, while the entire transept and part of the side aisles contain the complete cycle of the Life of Christ, from the annunciation of the coming of the Saviour, to Pentecost. Thus, just like a story unfolding, all the main events in the life of Jesus on earth can be seen in sequence: the baptism, the temptation, the judgement of Pilate, the ascent to Calvary, death, resurrection, and the most famous miracles - the feeding of the five thousand, healing the servant of a centurion, curing the stooped woman. The nave, being more distant from the symbolic heart of the cathedral, contains episodes that are also significant in the history of the church, though less important. Thus the stories of the Old Testament fill two entire bands, starting on the right wall of the nave. The scenes begin with the Creation and continue with the story of Adam and Eve in the Garden of Eden, their expulsion, the stories of Noah, Abraham, Lot, the destruction of Sodoma, and conclude with the image of Jacob wrestling with the angel. These mosaics are surrounded and enhanced by a myriad of secondary figures, in particu-

The Kiss of Judas Iscariot. *The suffocating crowd of soldiers lends movement and action to the scene.*

An interesting interpretation of the Crucifixion *in which the individual expressions are particularly intense.*

Following pages: the Ascent of Christ to Heaven, *with apostles and the Virgin Mary, flanked by two Angels.*

lar in the area of the apse and presbytery, though also dotted throughout the church, sometimes represented as full figures, sometimes as busts in fine medallions, often located in the underside of the arches. There are many images of Christ, as well as the Apostles, Angels, Saints, Martyrs, Doctors of the Church, Prophets, Hermits and even William II himself, portrayed twice - once above the royal throne, receiving his crown from Christ, and again just opposite, offering his cathedral to the Blessed Virgin. In addition to the images and figures are decorative mosaic features such as floral garlands, geometric designs, coloured borders and the ever-present acanthus, forming attractive frames and friezes. The glowing background is entirely golden, creating a brilliance and reflection of light which is quite unique.

Little is actually known about the craftsmen responsible for this masterpiece, though the matter has been discussed and debated at length. It is generally agreed that their inspiration was derived from Byzantine examples though there is a quite clear Romanesque influence. However, it is difficult to determine whether the craftsmen

who worked on the mosaics were local, or rather eastern or even Venetian. They were almost certainly completed by the end of the 12th century, though some extend this timing to the first half of the13th century. Though they do not, on the whole, demonstrate any great artistic flair or innovation, but rather imitative ability and technical skill, the artistry and beauty of these mosaics is exceptional. To remedy the inevitable damage and decay caused by time and man, much restoration has been carried out (unfortunately, not always with due care and respect) to preserve their glittering yet delicate beauty.

Saint Dominic and Saint Catherine.

THE CLOISTER

Apart from the cathedral, the buildings of the original monastery still in existence today are the royal palace, now a seminary, the refectory walls and in particular the splendid **cloister** flanking the south side of the church. Also commissioned by William II, in the second half of the 12th century, this magnificent example of Romanesque architecture forms a perfect square (each side measures 47 metres) enclosed by 228 pairs of columns, which form groups of four in the corners, with fine pointed arches rising from the capitals. It is fascinating to note that these elegant columns are all decorated with different designs and materials, from gold to mosaics, from precious stone to lava. The lovely decorative frieze above the arches is also made of limestone and lava. In the soffit of the arches and embedded into the structure, runs a grooved band which ends at the level of the capitals. It is thought that this unusual feature may once have served to hold wooden frames above the rectangular part of the arcading, protecting the monks from both heat and bad weather alike. The sculptures of the magnificent and imaginative capitals

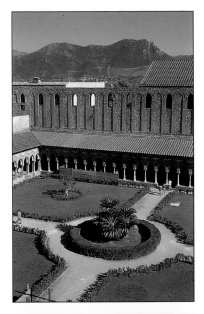

Views of the cloister showing the perfect harmony of this Romanesque masterpiece with a series of delicate paired columns.

Details showing the variety of decorative styles found in the cloisters.

are so fine and delicate that they appear to be engraved. An extensive gallery of characters and subjects is portrayed here, more even than those found in traditional medieval bestiaries, and consequently quite difficult to interpret. Illustrated here are biblical figures, pagan scenes, animals, allegories of the months, the classical acanthus leaves, cherubs and symbolic figures and inevitably William II portrayed offering the cathedral in homage to the Blessed Virgin. Little is known about the craftsmen; only one left his name to posterity, Romanus, son of Constantine, a marble worker who engraved his name on a capital on the north side of the cloister. In the south west corner a small square enclosure with three arches on each side forms a charming additional, inner **cloister** housing a delightful fountain which springs from a trunk with a stylized zig-zag design not unlike a palm tree. It is said that William II introduced the element of water, lending an oriental touch to this exquisite example of Sicilian art.

SICILIAN CUISINE

*T*here are two specific reasons behind the enormous variety of recipes that we find in Sicilian cuisine: geography and history. The island's geography was responsible for the great difficulty in communications between one part of Sicily and the other. Therefore, only local products were used in cooking. As to history, over the centuries Sicily had been invaded and conquered by many different civilizations each of which left a distinctive mark on the land and on its culinary traditions.

As a result of this great intermingling, we can find traces of the different populations in the ingredients and dishes which, over the years have been enriched and enhanced by Sicilian creativity.

Pasta cu li sardi
Pasta with Sardines

350g / 3/4lb bucatini (pasta straws)
500 - 600g / 1lb 2oz - 1lb 5oz fresh sardines (or sprats)
1 shallot (scallion)
Wild fennel tops
2 anchovies
Dried bread crumbs
Almonds, pine nuts, sultanas
Saffron
Olive oil

Soak a handful of sultanas in warm water. Toast a handful of skinned almonds in the oven and, in a frying pan, fry a generous handful of bread crumbs in a trickle of oil. Blanch a bunch of wild fennel leaves in plenty of salted water, keeping the water aside after draining the leaves. Clean the sardines, open them out flat and remove the heads and bones. Sauté the sliced onion together with the filleted sardines in 4-5 tablespoons of oil in the frying pan. When the sardines have dissolved, add the sultanas (squeezed of excess moisture), a tablespoon of pine nuts and a sachet of saffron. Season with salt, stir and allow the flavours to blend. Then add the chopped-up fennel tops and the sardines (keep 4 or 5 as a garnish).

Boil the pasta in the water the fennel has been cooked in, adding a pinch of saffron. Drain while still firm to the bite, dress with the sauce and sprinkle with bread crumbs. Transfer to an oven dish, garnish with the whole sardines, chopped almonds and a trickle of oil. Bake in the oven at 200°C / 44°F / Gas Mark 6 for 10 minutes.

Piscispata arrustutu
Grilled Sword Fish

4 sword fish steaks, 1kg / 2 1/4lb
Sammurigghiu sauce

Grill the lightly-oiled and salted fish (3-4 minutes each side) over red-hot charcoal. An electric grill may also be used. Serve immediately at the dinner table, together with the warm *sammurigghiu* sauce, prepared with garlic, oil, oregano, parsley, lemon juice, salt and pepper.

Sammurigghiu
Oregano Sauce

2 cloves of garlic   Parsley
2 lemons   Olive oil
Fresh oregano

Pour a glass (half-cup) of oil into a saucepan. Add half a glass of hot water and the juice of a lemon a little at a time, beating it all in with a fork or metal whisk. Season with salt and pepper. Then add a full tablespoon of fresh oregano, a small bunch of chopped parsley and the crushed garlic.
Simmer the sauce in a bain-marie (water bath) for 8-10 minutes. Transfer to a warmed dish and take to the dinner table. It is ideal to accompany dishes of baked fish. If you prefer something richer, amalgamate the pulp of 2-3 grilled tomatoes from which the seeds have been removed and which have also been blended in the electric blender.

Sardi a beccaficu
Stuffed Sardines

1kg / 21/4lb fresh sardines
(or sprats)
4 salted anchovies
1 lemon
Dried bread crumbs

Sultanas
Bay leaves, parsley
Granulated sugar
Olive oil
Pine nuts

Rinse the sardines under running water and trim them, discarding the heads and bones. Open them out flat and allow to drain, one on top of the other.

Toast a couple of generous handfuls of dried bread crumbs in 3-4 tablespoons of oil in a frying pan. In a bowl, mix with the anchovies, broken up and cleaned of all little bones, a sprig of parsley (chopped), a handful of soaked sultanas (squeezed of excess moisture), a handful of pine nuts, salt and pepper.

Stuff the sardines with the mixture and close them up. Lay them in a greased oven dish, each one separated by a bay leaf. Sprinkle over the bread crumbs, dress with a little oil and the lemon juice in which a teaspoon of sugar has been dissolved. Bake in a pre-heated oven at 180°C / 350°F / Gas Mark 4 for half-an-hour. Take out and serve.

Tunnina ca cipuddata
Tuna fish, onion and vinegar

4 tuna fish steaks (800g / 13/4lb)	Flour
1 onion	White wine vinegar
Parsley	Olive oil

Coat the tuna fish steaks with flour. Brown in 4-5 tablespoons of oil in a frying pan. Drain and keep warm. Soften the sliced onion in 4-5 tablespoons of oil in a saucepan. Souse with a scant glass (scant half-cup) of vinegar, then add the fish. Allow the flavours to be absorbed briefly. Add the onion and a sprig of parsley, all chopped up. Check the seasoning of salt and pepper, sprinkle a little vinegar over and serve. A tasty dish which can be eaten either hot or cold.

Caponata
Aubergine (Eggplant) Stew

800g / 13/4lb Aubergines (eggplant)

Capers	Pine nuts
3 celery stalks	Granulated sugar
2 onions	Vinegar
2-3 tomatoes	Fresh Basil, olive oil
120g / 4oz / 3/4 cup green olives, stoned	

Clean and slice the aubergines (eggplant). Place on a tray, sprinkle with coarse salt and leave under a weight for about an hour until the bitter liquid runs out of the vegetable. Meanwhile, trim the celery and blanch it in lightly-salted water for five minutes. Drain, cut into chunks and brown gently in a little oil in a frying pan. Set aside.

Peel the onion, slice finely and let it colour in 3-4 tablespoons of oil in a frying pan, together with the rinsed capers, the olives and a handful of pine nuts. Add

the skinned, seeded tomatoes, cut to pieces. Allow the flavours to blend over gentle heat (20').

Rinse, dry and dice the aubergines. Brown in 4-5 tablespoons of boiling oil in the frying pan.

As soon as they turn golden, toss in the celery and the onion and tomato sauce. Stir and let the flavours marry over a gentle flame (20'), adjusting the salt.

Add a teaspoon of sugar and a liqueur glass of vinegar. Allow to evaporate almost completely. Draw off the heat, garnish with a sprig of basil and leave to cool before serving. Caponata will keep in the refrigerator for a few days.

'Nzalata d'aranci
Orange Salad

6 oranges (preferably not too ripe)
2-3 sprigs of parsley
Olive oil

Peel the oranges and remove the white pith. Separate the segments one by one and cut to pieces, stripping them of the skin covering them. Arrange on a serving dish and sprinkle with some chopped parsley. Dress the salad with a trickle of olive oil, a little salt and a grinding of black pepper. This is a delicacy to accompany roast meat.

INDEX